Hello, Slider™!

The *Cleveland Indians*™ Mascot

Bob Feller

Miguel De Angel with Justin Hilton

MASCOT BOOKS®

www.mascotbooks.com

Slider, the *Cleveland Indians* mascot, was on his way to the ballpark for a baseball game.

As he approached the ballpark, a group
of Indians fans cheered, "Hello, Slider!"

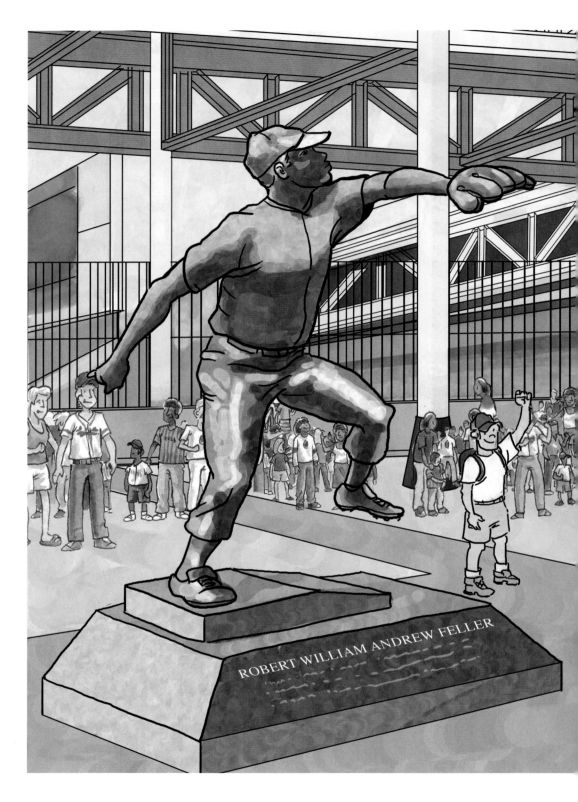

Slider's first stop was the statue
of Bob Feller, one of the greatest
baseball players of all time.

While he was admiring the statue, Slider
was surprised by a friendly voice that
called, "Hello, Slider!" It was Bob Feller!

Slider arrived at the ballpark in time for batting
practice. The Indians wore their blue batting
practice jerseys as they took practice swings.

Slider walked into the batting cage and gave an Indians player a few helpful tips. With Slider's help, the player hit several balls out of the ballpark. The batter said, "Thank you, Slider!"

After batting practice, the ballpark grounds crew went to work. With great pride, they quickly prepared the field for play.

The batting cage was removed, the
lines were chalked, and the infield
was raked. As the grounds crew
worked, they cheered, "Hello, Slider!"

With the start of the game only moments away, Slider was feeling hungry. He grabbed some snacks and an Indians pennant at the concession stands.

As he made his way back to the field,
a family cheered, "Hello, Slider!"

It was now time for player introductions and the National Anthem. Slider joined the team on the third base line.

Slider and the players gazed at the American
Flag as four military planes flew overhead.
The players called, "Hello, Slider!"

The umpire yelled, "PLAY BALL!"
and the first batter stepped to the
plate. It was time for the first pitch.

The Indians pitcher delivered a perfect fastball. "STRIKE ONE!" called the umpire.

Slider made his way into the stands to
visit with some of his friends and fans.

Slider's silly antics made everyone
laugh. Fans nearby cheered,
"Hello, Slider!"

It was now time for the seventh
inning stretch and the singing of
Take Me Out to the Ballgame™!

Fans sang arm-in-arm as Slider led the crowd. Afterwards, Indians fans cheered, "Hello, Slider!"

The Indians trailed by one run in the bottom of the ninth inning. With a runner on first base, the team's best player stepped to the plate.

With a powerful swing, the batter launched
a home run! A lucky fan caught the ball as
it landed in the stands. The crowd cheered,
"Indians win! Indians win!"

Cleveland Indians fans celebrated the
thrilling victory. Slider left the ballpark
and headed for home.

It had been a long day at the ballpark.
Slider crawled into bed and fell fast asleep.
Good night, Slider!

About the Author

This farm boy from Van Meter, Iowa, was only 17 when he struck out eight members of the *St. Louis Cardinals*™ in three innings of an exhibition game. He originally signed a contract with the *Cleveland Indians*™ in 1935 to play in Fargo, North Dakota with the Indians Farm Club in the Northern League. After his performance against the Cardinals, instead of reporting to Fargo, the Indians sent him to Philadelphia to join the *Major League*™ team. As a rookie, he struck out 17 batters in a single game, which at that time was an *American League*™ record. In 1940, he became the only Major League pitcher to throw a no-hitter on opening day.

At age 23, his career was interrupted by his four-year enlistment in the Navy. Upon entering the Navy, Feller attended War College and became a gun captain aboard the battleship U.S.S. Alabama and came out a highly decorated war veteran with eight Battle Stars and five campaign ribbons. He then re-entered *Major League Baseball*® to regain his dominance on the mound. Even though his military career consumed four prime baseball years, Feller ranks 28th in history with 266 wins. He remains the Indians all-time leader in shutouts (46), strikeouts (2,581), innings (3,827) and *All-Star Game*® appearances (8).

To this day, baseball historians speculate that Bob Feller might have won 100 more games and recorded nearly 1,000 to 1,200 more strikeouts had he not joined the Navy. Also, he may have pitched other no-hitters or 1 hitters and broken other records that would have stood for decades. In 1962, Feller was inducted into the National Baseball Hall of Fame on the first ballot.

Hey Kids! Become part of the team by joining the Cleveland Indians Kids' Club for all kids ages 14 and under. For more information, call 216-420-HITS or log on to: **www.indians.com**.

For more information about our products, please visit us online at www.mascotbooks.com.

Mascot Books, Inc. - P.O. Box 220157, Chantilly, VA 20153-0157

Major League Baseball trademarks and copyrights are used
with permission of Major League Baseball Properties, Inc. MLB.com

ISBN: 978-1-932888-88-1
Printed in the United States.
www.mascotbooks.com

MLB

Boston Red Sox™
Hello, Wally!
by Jerry Remy

*Wally And His Journey
Through Red Sox Nation™*
by Jerry Remy

New York Yankees™
Let's Go, Yankees™!
by Yogi Berra

New York Mets™
Hello, Mr. Met™!
by Rusty Staub

St. Louis Cardinals™
Hello, Fredbird™!
by Ozzie Smith

Chicago Cubs™
Let's Go, Cubs™!
by Aimee Aryal

Chicago White Sox™
Let's Go, White Sox™!
by Aimee Aryal

Philadelphia Phillies™
Hello, Phillie Phanatic™!
by Aimee Aryal

Cleveland Indians™
Hello, Slider™!
by Bob Feller

NBA

Dallas Mavericks
Let's Go, Mavs!
by Mark Cuban

NFL

Dallas Cowboys
How 'Bout Them Cowboys
by Aimee Aryal

More Coming Soon

Collegiate

Auburn University
War Eagle! by Pat Dye
Hello, Aubie! by Aimee Aryal

Boston College
Hello, Baldwin! by Aimee Aryal

Brigham Young University
Hello, Cosmo!
by Pat and LaVell Edwards

Clemson University
Hello, Tiger! by Aimee Aryal

Duke University
Hello, Blue Devil! by Aimee Aryal

Florida State University
Let's Go 'Noles! by Aimee Aryal

Georgia Tech
Hello, Buzz! by Aimee Aryal

Indiana University
Let's Go Hoosiers! by Aimee Aryal

James Madison University
Hello, Duke Dog! by Aimee Aryal

Kansas State University
Hello, Willie! by Dan Walter

Louisiana State University
Hello, Mike! by Aimee Aryal

Michigan State University
Hello, Sparty! by Aimee Aryal

Mississippi State University
Hello, Bully! by Aimee Aryal

North Carolina State University
Hello, Mr. Wuf! by Aimee Aryal

Penn State University
We Are Penn State by Joe Paterno
Hello, Nittany Lion! by Aimee Aryal

Purdue University
Hello, Purdue Pete! by Aimee Aryal

Rutgers University
Hello, Scarlet Knight! by Aimee Aryal

Syracuse University
Hello, Otto! by Aimee Aryal

Texas A&M
Howdy, Reveille! by Aimee Aryal

UCLA
Hello, Joe Bruin! by Aimee Aryal

University of Alabama
Roll Tide! by Kenny Stabler
Hello, Big Al! by Aimee Aryal

University of Arkansas
Hello, Big Red! By Aimee Aryal

University of Connecticut
Hello, Jonathan! by Aimee Aryal

University of Florida
Hello, Albert! by Aimee Aryal

University of Georgia
How 'Bout Them Dawgs!
by Vince Dooley
Hello, Hairy Dawg! by Aimee Aryal

University of Illinois
Let's Go, Illini! by Aimee Aryal

University of Iowa
Hello, Herky! by Aimee Aryal

University of Kansas
Hello, Big Jay! by Aimee Aryal

University of Kentucky
Hello, Wildcat! by Aimee Aryal

University of Maryland
Hello, Testudo! by Aimee Aryal

University of Michigan
Let's Go, Blue! by Aimee Aryal

University of Minnesota
Hello, Goldy! by Aimee Aryal

University of Mississippi
Hello, Colonel Rebel! by Aimee Aryal

University of Nebraska
Hello, Herbie Husker! by Aimee Aryal

University of North Carolina
Hello, Rameses! by Aimee Aryal

University of Notre Dame
Let's Go Irish! by Aimee Aryal

University of Oklahoma
Let's Go Sooners! by Aimee Aryal

University of South Carolina
Hello, Cocky! by Aimee Aryal

University of Southern California
Hello, Tommy Trojan! by Aimee Aryal

University of Tennessee
Hello, Smokey! by Aimee Aryal

University of Texas
Hello, Hook 'Em! by Aimee Aryal

University of Virginia
Hello, CavMan! by Aimee Aryal

University of Wisconsin
Hello, Bucky! by Aimee Aryal

Virginia Tech
Yea, It's Hokie Game Day!
by Cheryl and Frank Beamer
Hello, Hokie Bird! by Aimee Aryal

Wake Forest University
Hello, Demon Deacon!
by Aimee Aryal

West Virginia University
Hello, Mountaineer! by Aimee Aryal

NHL

Coming Soon

Visit us online at www.mascotbooks.com for a complete list of titles.